W9-ARN-923

HAUNTED HOUSES

by Jason Friedman

FOR MY PARENTS

Special thanks to Richard S. Broughton, Ph.D., and the staff of the Institute for Parapsychology at the Foundation for Research on the Nature of Man, for reference assistance and for introducing me to parapsychology. Thanks also to Joanne D.S. McMahon, Ph.D., of the Parapsychology Foundation's Eileen Garrett Library, for enabling my understanding of Garrett and of modern ghostbusting.

Published by The Trumpet Club
666 Fifth Avenue, New York, New York 10103

ISBN 0-440-84641-2

Printed in the United States of America
October 1992
1   3   5   7   9   10   8   6   4   2
CWO

PHOTOGRAPH CREDITS

p. 43: © AP/Wide World Photos. *p. 44: top,* © Bettmann/Hulton; *bottom,* © Culver Pictures. *p. 45: top,* © Mary Evans/Harry Price Coll., Univ. of London; *bottom,* © Bettmann/Hulton. *p. 46: top,* © Mary Evans/Harry Price Coll., Univ. of London; *bottom,* © Bettmann/Hulton. *p. 47: top, bottom,* © Winchester Mystery House Historical Museum. *p. 48: top,* © The Bettmann Archive; *bottom,* © UPI/Bettmann. *p. 49: top,* © Mary Evans/Harry Price Coll., Univ. of London; *bottom,* © AP/Wide World Photos. *p. 50:* © Mary Evans/Harry Price Coll., Univ. of London.

Cover: © Mary Evans/Harry Price Coll., Univ. of London

Contents

Introduction

Have you ever heard strange creaks or groans that you can't explain in your house? Have lights flicked on or off without anyone touching a switch? Maybe you've felt cold blasts of air even when all the windows were shut, or your dog suddenly started to bark for no apparent reason. If these things have happened to you, some people might say your house is haunted!

Why would a ghost haunt a particular house? One reason, some say, is that spirits return to places that were important to them while they were alive. Maybe they loved the place—maybe they hated it—or something could have happened in the house that the spirits can't forget. Another popular idea is that when people die suddenly, leaving unfinished business, their spirits return. Still another theory is that ghosts living in haunted houses have messages they want to deliver to the living.

You may not believe in ghosts or haunted houses. But many people throughout history *have* believed in them. In the 19th century some people actually tried to communicate with the spirit world. *Spiritualists,* as they came to be known, believed only certain people could speak to ghosts. These people, who claim they can communicate with the spirit world, are called *mediums*. Mediums are thought to see, feel, and hear things nobody else can. Even today, if people think their houses are haunted, they will sometimes call in a medium to talk to the ghosts and try to find out why the spirits can't rest.

Scientists are still trying to find out whether ghosts exist. These scientists, called *parapsychologists,* study supernatural events like reports of ghosts and hauntings. They attempt to understand and explain these events using scientific means.

But can science explain the legend of England's Borley Rectory, where a nun is said to have been buried alive—only to come back to walk the garden paths? Or the reason why a widow built the largest mansion in the United States, so the ghosts who haunted her would have a place to stay?

Can a house be haunted? Do spirits return to a particular place after death? Can we communicate with these spirits? Or are there other explanations for hauntings?

Some of the stories you will read here have been told for centuries. Some of the events were reported much more recently. Did ghosts really haunt these houses? Read this book and decide for yourself!

1

Historical Haunted Houses

The Tower of London in England . . . the White House in Washington, D.C. . . . the U.S. Military Academy at West Point in New York State. People from all over the world come to visit these famous sites—places where kings and queens and presidents and generals have lived. Places where history has been made. Places you can visit today. Places that, some say, are haunted!

The Tower of London

England's Tower of London was built nearly 1,000 years ago. It's a huge fortress made of cold, gray stone and filled with houses, towers, and yards. Today the Tower of London is a popular tourist attraction, but for hundreds of years it was a fearsome prison with a bloody history. Thousands of people— from common criminals to kings and queens—were executed in the Tower. As legend has it, many of their spirits still haunt it.

In 1483 two young princes were brought to the Tower and thrown into prison. Twelve-year-old Edward V was the new young king and his 10-year-old brother Richard, Duke of York, was next in line to the throne. But their uncle, Richard III, wanted to rule England. He had the young princes locked up in the Tower and, many believe, secretly murdered. Nobody knows for certain what happened, but the boys disappeared and were never seen again.

For the next 200 years, many people claimed they saw the princes' ghosts. The boys were always reported to be wearing nightgowns, walking hand in hand through the Tower grounds. Then, in 1674, workmen found skeletons of two young boys in a wooden chest. Did the bones belong to the brothers? No one knew for sure, but the skeletons were given a royal burial. No one has seen the princes' ghosts since.

Maybe the best-known spirit thought to haunt the Tower is the ghost of Anne Boleyn. Anne, the second wife of King Henry VIII, was beheaded in 1536. Henry had divorced his first wife to marry Anne. Now Henry wanted to marry a third time. (Altogether he had six wives!) So he decided to have Anne arrested, then executed.

Anne has been reported walking through the Tower halls—with and without her head—sometimes leading a ghostly group of lords and ladies and sometimes walking alone. In 1864 one of the guards claimed he saw a woman dressed in white come out of the room where Anne had spent her last night. "Halt!" he said. But the woman kept moving. Finally, the guard stabbed her with the bayonet of his rifle.

Nothing happened—the bayonet went right through her, as if she were made of air. The guard was so terrified, he fainted on the spot. Other guards said they, too, had seen this phantom lady. Everyone agreed it must be the ghost of Anne Boleyn.

But perhaps the most gruesome sightings reported are those of the Countess of Salisbury. She was beheaded in 1541—also at the order of Henry VIII, who thought she wanted to remove him from his throne. The Countess was 70 years old at the time. At first she somehow managed to escape the executioner. But he chased her around the Tower yard with an ax until finally she was caught. People say they see that same scene played out—in ghostly form—every May 27. That's the day the Countess died.

Hampton Court

Just outside of London is Hampton Court. It was once the royal residence of Henry VIII. Now it's another tourist attraction, with more than its share of ghost stories. There have been reports of a White Lady and a Gray Lady ghost, and several claims that two of Henry's wives still haunt the palace grounds.

Henry's third wife, Jane Seymour, died in 1537, one week after giving birth to their son. Each year on her son's birthday she is said to roam the halls, carrying a lighted candle and searching for something—or someone—she'll never find.

The ghost of Henry's fifth wife, Catherine Howard, has been reported so often she's listed in the tourist guidebook! In 1542 Henry had Catherine arrested for treason. But the night before she was to be beheaded, Catherine escaped from her guards. She ran screaming through the halls of Hampton Court, pleading for her life. Henry ignored her cries, and the next day she was executed. Every year on the anniversary of her death, February 13, Catherine is said to run sobbing through those same halls, known today as the Haunted Gallery.

Years later an artist was drawing a picture in the Haunted Gallery. He looked up from his pad and saw a hand stretch out from behind a tapestry. Quickly, the artist sketched the hand—wearing a ring—before it disappeared. Later, experts were called in to examine the picture. They said the ring had belonged to Catherine Howard.

The White House

Does the President of the United States live in a haunted house? Many people think the White House —with its graceful columns, well-kept gardens, and beautiful fountains, right in the heart of Washington, D.C.—*is* haunted.

Ghosts have often been reported in the White House. Dolley Madison, the wife of the fourth President, James Madison, was said to have appeared over 100 years after her death in 1849. During the term of Woodrow Wilson (1913–1921), twenty-eighth President of the United States, gardeners were about to dig up the rose garden that Mrs. Madison had planted when she was living in the White House because Mrs. Wilson wanted the roses removed. But the gardeners stopped digging when they saw Dolley Madison's ghost. She told them to keep it exactly the way she had planted it. The White House rose garden hasn't been changed since.

Many visitors to the White House claim to have heard footsteps echoing in empty halls and strange knockings in the middle of the night. Many people believe it is the ghost of the sixteenth President, Abraham Lincoln.

Lincoln was assassinated on April 14, 1865. The Civil War had just ended and Lincoln still had much work to do. The country needed him. Some people believed Lincoln's spirit knew that. So immediately after his death, stories sprang up about his ghost roaming the White House halls.

It wasn't until Calvin Coolidge took office in 1923, though, that Lincoln's ghost was actually sighted. First Lady Grace Coolidge said she saw a tall, thin figure staring out a window in the Oval Office. That room was thought to be Lincoln's favorite place in the White House.

Then, during the presidency of Franklin Delano Roosevelt, more sightings were reported. One afternoon in the early 1940's, a White House secretary dashed into President Roosevelt's office. She was frightened—she said she had just seen Lincoln's ghost! He was sitting in his old bedroom, she claimed, pulling on a pair of boots.

Not long after, another mysterious sighting was related by Queen Wilhemina of the Netherlands. She was staying at the White House as a guest of President Roosevelt and his wife, Eleanor. Late one night, the Queen was getting ready for bed when she heard a knock on the door. Surprised that someone would disturb her so late at night, she quickly threw open the door. There in the hall, she later said, was Abraham Lincoln, standing well over 6 feet tall, wearing his famous stovepipe hat! Queen Wilhemina gasped in shock. As she stood there trembling, the image of Lincoln faded and disappeared. After she was sure the ghost had gone, Queen Wilhemina crept back into bed. But she slept uneasily, thinking that Lincoln might once again appear.

Some people say that Queen Wilhemina was a great believer in ghosts. She might have *wanted* to see Abraham Lincoln so much that she convinced herself she had. But even today visitors complain of strange sounds and weird feelings. So who knows what ghostly sights a White House tour might include?

West Point

The U.S. Military Academy at West Point, built in New York State in 1802 to train young men to become army officers, is a truly historic site. (West Point now accepts women as well.) With its dark, ivy-covered buildings, it's easy to imagine ghosts wandering the grounds.

One West Point phantom—who isn't very scary—is

said to be the ghost of a housekeeper named Molly. She worked for Superintendent Sylvanus Thayer between 1817 and 1832, and lived in Quarters 100, which is in the basement. The current superintendent and his family still live in that house today. The basement, though, has been restored; now it looks as it did in Molly's time. It is kept as a museum for tour groups to visit—nobody lives there. Why is it, then, that the breadboard in the kitchen is always damp? It's as if Molly has just finished kneading bread. And why is one of the beds often rumpled in the mornings? Has Molly's ghost just woken up? Nobody knows. But cadets still camp out there all night, hoping to see her.

A scarier ghost was reported in October 1972. Two cadets were sleeping in their dormitory, room 4714 of the 47th Division Barracks. Suddenly, one cadet was awakened by a strange sound. He noticed a ghostly figure walking through the door. Quickly, he tried to wake up his roommate. But by then the figure had disappeared. Different cadets took turns sleeping in the room, hoping they'd find out if the ghost was real. Some men had a strange feeling while they were there, and others felt very cold. And some thought nothing at all was out of the ordinary. But a few other cadets claimed to see the figure, too. They all described him as a soldier with a handlebar mustache, wearing an old-fashioned uniform.

These cadets did some research in the West Point library. They discovered that the dorm was near the spot where an officer's house had burned down about

100 years before. The officer had died in the fire. Had the cadets seen his spirit? Maybe, maybe not. Later, a student at a rival school admitted the whole incident had been a Halloween prank. But some people thought *he* was lying—they didn't believe this sort of prank was possible. And to this day, there is talk of the ghostly soldier in room 4714.

2

Haunted House Legends

In every part of the world, legends of ghosts and haunted houses are passed down from generation to generation. And with each generation, there are new reports of ghostly sightings. Do people imagine these ghosts they've heard so much about? Or do they really see them?

The Haunting of Grey House

Nearly 150 years ago, Mr. and Mrs. M. Divorne and their six children moved into Grey House, a dark, gloomy-looking mansion about 50 miles from Paris, France. Mr. Divorne, a salesman, wanted to leave the hustle and bustle of the capital. He was looking forward to growing fresh vegetables in the peaceful countryside. The real estate agent hadn't told the Divornes that people in their new neighborhood thought Grey House was haunted. There were rumors of mysterious deaths, and people complained that they felt cold whenever they walked past the house. And for years there were stories of people moving into the house, only to pack up their things right away and move back out.

Mrs. Divorne did have a strange feeling when she first walked into Grey House. Inside, the house was eerie-looking, with many stairways leading to dark, musty rooms. Even after adding paint and cheerful wallpaper, Mrs. Divorne still felt something was wrong with the enormous old house. And it didn't take long for her children to agree.

A few weeks after the family moved in, Louise, one of the older daughters, woke up from a sound sleep. It was still dark out. The Divornes' dogs were barking wildly downstairs. Suddenly, Louise heard the sound of a heavy object being rolled down the stairs near her bedroom. She was more curious than frightened, so she jumped out of bed and opened her door—but nothing was there! The thumping sound grew louder as it made its way downstairs.

Louise heard more noises—the sound of dishes being broken! Then—dead silence. Terrified, Louise ran back to her bedroom and locked the door.

A few days later two servants smelled something terrible coming from one of the kitchen drains. No one knew what the smell was. Mr. Divorne had checked all the plumbing before they moved in, and everything was supposedly in good condition. Before long, one of the Divornes' sons, Henri, smelled the horrible odor, too. As it was getting dark one evening, Henri was standing at his bedroom window, lost in thought, gazing at the gardens below. In the next instant, his daydreams were shattered. The dogs started to bark right outside his door, and suddenly Henri felt very cold. Then a powerful odor surrounded him—it smelled like something rotting—and Henri felt sick. He threw open his bedroom window and gulped deep breaths of fresh air. Then he heard a noise behind him. When he turned around he saw a tall shape moving across the room! The shape disappeared, but Henri was still terrified. He ran downstairs and told the rest of his family what had happened.

Mrs. Divorne and the children became frightened. They wanted to move out right then and there. But Mr. Divorne liked the house, and decided the family should stay there.

One beautiful, clear day, two of the girls were taking a walk on one of the garden paths. Suddenly, Marie had the feeling they were being followed. She spun around to look, but nobody was behind them. The feeling would not go away, so the two sisters headed back toward the house. Soon they came to an ancient well that had been closed up many years before. As they paused to look at it, they felt something rush past them. Then they heard a loud splash, as if a heavy object had fallen into the well. Marie and Henriette were so frightened that they started to run. As they ran, the girls heard footsteps pounding down the path after them!

Later that same day the servants quit. They said they couldn't stand the awful noises and bad smells any longer. Then Henriette became very sick, and the doctor couldn't figure out what was wrong. Mrs.

Divorne begged her husband to sell the house, but he wanted to wait a little longer. Toward the end of November, only two months after the family had moved in, the weather turned raw and rainy. Mr. Divorne was not feeling well and decided to go to bed early. A storm blew through the trees and the wind whistled in the chimneys. But Mr. Divorne was so tired that he quickly fell asleep.

Suddenly, his eyes flew open. There was a horrible stench in the room. And standing at the foot of his bed was a rotting corpse! The decaying flesh was falling off the bones. The wrinkled lips were pulled into a horrible grin, showing long yellow teeth. Mr. Divorne fainted. When he woke up, the room was dark and the awful ghost had vanished. The next morning he told his grateful family that he would sell the house as soon as possible.

The Divornes were able to sell Grey House without any problems. They moved into a new home, Henriette got well again, and life went back to normal.

But Pierre, the Divornes' teenage son, wanted to know more about their old house. He decided to find out its history. Soon Pierre discovered that Grey House was the third house to be built on that piece of land. A bloody murder had taken place in the first house and, since then, the land was said to be cursed.

That first house had burned down in a mysterious fire. A second house was built, only to be destroyed in 1789 during the French Revolution. At that time, some people in France were very rich, but most people were very poor. The wealthy treated those without money almost like slaves—they had very few rights. During the Revolution, the poor rebelled against the wealthy, including the owners of Grey House. People tore through the rooms, attacking anyone who was home. Everyone was thrown down the well—even if they were still alive! Did these drowned souls come back to tell the Divornes how they had died? Maybe they wanted to make sure *nobody* ever lived in their house! Whatever the reason, the haunting of Grey House is a legend that endures to this day.

The Most Haunted House in England

Since the 13th century, villagers in the quiet town of Borley have reported seeing the ghostly figure of a nun on the same day every year. She appears at the place where an ancient *monastery* (a community of monks) once stood. Legend has it that this nun from a nearby *convent* (a community of nuns) fell in love with a monk from the monastery. They planned to elope, even though nuns and monks are forbidden by religious law to marry. But they were caught before they could leave the monastery grounds. The monk was hanged. The nun was forced to stand in one corner of the convent basement, while a brick wall was built around her to make sure she didn't escape. Supposedly she was left to die. It is believed she died sometime during the 13th century on July 28, the day she appears every year.

In 1863 the Reverend Henry Bull built Borley Rectory directly on the site of that ancient monastery. (A *rectory* is the house where the neighborhood clergyman, or *rector*, lives.) At that time there were hundreds of rectories in England. But this one was different—people believed *this* rectory was haunted.

Almost as soon as they moved in, the Reverend Henry Bull and his family reported seeing the nun. When the Reverend died in 1892, his son Harry became rector of the neighborhood and moved back into his childhood home with his wife and children. On July 28, 1900, three of Harry's sisters—Ethel, Freda, and Mabel—saw the nun again.

The three sisters were coming back from a garden party in the late afternoon. They were laughing and talking. When they reached the rectory gate, they suddenly became quiet. On the other side of the gate, gliding down the garden path, was a shrouded figure that looked like a nun!

For a moment the sisters were too frightened to move. Then Freda ran inside to get Elsie, a fourth sister. Elsie came out and started walking toward the ghostly nun—she wanted to ask what the ghost wanted. But as soon as she got close, the ghost disappeared!

From time to time, the Reverend Harry Bull and his family said they saw the ghostly nun. They heard unexplained sounds, too. Once, late at night, the whole family was awakened by the bells of the rectory ringing loudly—though no one was pulling them! The Reverend Harry Bull was afraid of the

16

mysterious bell-ringing. He thought it meant that evil spirits haunted the rectory grounds. But he didn't want to frighten his family.

So the Reverend Harry Bull told all sorts of jokes about ghosts to make his family less afraid. Once he told them that after he died, *he* was going to haunt the rectory. They would know it was he, he said, because his ghost would always throw mothballs. After he died in 1927, some workers in the house claimed that they saw mothballs flying around the Reverend's old bedroom! Some people even claimed to see the Reverend Harry Bull's ghost walking around the room in an old gray bedjacket.

The Reverend Eric Smith and his wife moved into Borley Rectory soon after Harry Bull's death. The Smiths reported that lights flickered on and off, all by themselves. Pebbles flew at the windows, strange footsteps were heard in the hall, but no one was there! Once Mr. Smith heard a woman's voice crying out near the chapel: "Don't, Carlos, don't!" The woman sounded as if she were in pain. Mr. Smith ran to the chapel, but he didn't see anyone there.

The Smiths became afraid to close their eyes at night. Finally, they contacted the London *Daily Mirror* for help. On June 12, 1929, a reporter from the newspaper visited Borley Rectory. The reporter brought along Harry Price, England's most famous ghost hunter at the time. Price stayed at Borley Rectory for 3 days. He claimed he saw the nun in the garden and heard many of the mysterious noises. When he left, Harry Price was convinced that Borley

17

Rectory was the most haunted house in England. The Smiths then decided to move out.

But the rectory didn't stay empty for long. And the most horrifying disturbances were still to come. In October 1930 the Reverend L. A. Foyster and his wife, Marianne, moved in. Almost at once, they reported strange incidents. First an invisible hand struck Marianne in the face. Some nights she was thrown out of bed. Once she claimed that her own mattress had tried to smother her! Crooked writing appeared on little pieces of paper and on the walls of the rectory. These messages seemed to be asking for help. They read "Prayers," "Mass," and "Light." Objects appeared out of thin air—only to disappear immediately!

The Foysters left Borley Rectory after 5 years in the house. Things quieted down during their final 3 years there—not much happened to them.

But Harry Price had not forgotten the most haunted house in England. He moved in with a team of investigators. Price claimed to see the ghostly nun many times. He also noticed strange smells and freezing temperatures inside the house. In 1939 the house burned down in a mysterious fire. After that, Price dug in the cellar—and found the skeleton of a young woman! Were these the remains of the nun who had been buried alive—and whose unhappy spirit was said to wander the rooms and grounds of Borley Rectory?

In the 1940's Harry Price published two books, *The Most Haunted House in England* and *The End of*

Borley Rectory. Many people believed that Price was a fake. One newspaper reporter said he had caught Price setting up strange disturbances. And other experts thought that Price was lying or exaggerating. People have written that the Bulls saw what they expected to see—and what they *wanted* to see! As an elderly woman, Ethel Bull, one of the sisters who said she had seen the nun, admitted that nothing strange had ever happened in the rectory. Marianne Foyster later said that the house was haunted only by bats, rats, the wind—and the neighborhood boys who threw stones. But the ghost stories live on. And people still talk about the most haunted house in England.

The Winchester Mystery House

A rich widow named Sarah Winchester was so afraid of ghosts she built a house—just for them. Her mansion still stands. It is one of the most famous haunted houses in the United States.

It all began 130 years ago. In 1862, just before she was to be married, Sarah Parlee went to a fortune-teller. The fortune-teller gave her a warning: "Beware your future husband and the souls of the people his family has destroyed. They will come back to haunt you."

Sarah Parlee didn't listen to the fortune-teller—she married William Winchester anyway. He owned the Winchester Repeating Arms Company—and his father had invented the famous Winchester rifle.

Years went by and Sarah Winchester was happy. Then tragedy struck. First her child died; then, within a year, on March 7, 1881, her husband died of tuberculosis. Some people say Sarah Winchester never got over her grief, and that she went crazy with loneliness. In 1881 Sarah went to a séance. She wanted to contact her husband's spirit.

At the séance, the medium told Sarah that her husband wanted her to build a big house. Who would live there? Sarah asked. The medium answered, The ghosts of all the people who had been killed by Winchester guns!

The medium convinced Sarah Winchester that the ghosts were angry. People were dying every day from Winchester guns. They needed a place to go—a big place with lots of room.

Sarah believed the medium. Quickly she sold her Connecticut home and moved to California. When she was passing through San Jose, in northern California about 40 miles south of San Francisco, she saw a mansion under construction. Something told her that this was the perfect house for her plan, so she bought it.

For 36 years, 7 days a week, Sarah Winchester kept building and changing the house. She added rooms, then tore them down. She built staircases that didn't lead anywhere and doors that opened onto brick walls. She installed elevators that went up only one floor—even though at one time the house was seven stories high! The outside looked just as strange. Towers rose up from some corners but not others. Pointy spires stuck up from the middle of the roof. Today, the Winchester Mystery House has 160 rooms and is the largest private home in the United States. But the mansion looks like ten different houses all stuck together!

Sarah Winchester held séances in the windowless Blue Room to ask the spirits their building instructions. She even held dinner parties for the ghosts. But she also thought the ghosts might be too angry to accept her good will, and she was afraid. She decided to trick them with winding hallways and dead ends. She hoped the ghosts would have a hard time finding her. Just to make sure, Sarah Winchester spent every night in a different bedroom!

On April 18, 1906, Sarah Winchester was sleeping in the Daisy Room, a bedroom that had flower patterns in its stained glass window. Suddenly, she felt the house start to shake. It was the great San Francisco earthquake! The top three floors of the house collapsed, and Sarah Winchester found herself trapped beneath a caved-in ceiling. Finally she was rescued. She refused ever to go into the Daisy Room again, but it is said her spirit still haunts it. Once visitors even claimed that they felt the room shake violently, just as it had during the earthquake.

Sarah Winchester died in 1922, at the age of 85. Today the Winchester Mystery House is a popular attraction for tourists who want to see the world's *only* palace built for ghosts!

3

Famous Mediums

In 1848, for the first time, two people claimed that they had actually talked to a ghost. Sisters Margaretta and Kate Fox were the first mediums—people who say they can communicate with ghosts. The spiritualism movement—the belief that people *can* talk to the spirits of the dead—had begun.

The Fox sisters' fame spread quickly. Soon they were showing other people how to contact spirits, and there were hundreds of mediums all over the world. These first mediums held séances in which small groups of people gathered around a table in a dark room and called on spirits to talk with them. There are still people who hold séances today.

The Fox Family Ghost

Margaretta and Kate Fox lived with their parents in a little house in Hydesville, New York. In March 1848, when Margaretta was 15 years old and Kate was 11, Mr. and Mrs. Fox heard strange knocking and banging noises coming from their daughters' bedroom every night. The Foxes were frightened and went to investigate. They couldn't figure out where the strange sounds were coming from, so they decided a ghost must be making the noises. Since the sounds weren't hurting anyone, the family got used to them.

One night, soon after the knocking sounds began, Margaretta and Kate decided to knock back. To the sisters' surprise, their raps were returned. They called excitedly to their parents, who came running into the girls' bedroom. Margaretta and Kate told the spirit to rap two times for no and three times for yes. Then the girls began asking the spirit questions. Standing in the doorway, Mr. and Mrs. Fox could hardly believe what they were hearing. The ghost—if that's what it was—was answering!

Over the next few days, Margaretta and Kate questioned the spirit for many hours. The girls figured out that the spirit could spell out words by rapping. They made up a code: a certain number of raps for each letter of the alphabet. When the girls put the letters together, they spelled words. The ghost first spelled out his name—Charles Rosa.

Charles Rosa was a peddler who had stopped at the house one afternoon in 1844 and was never seen again. Next the girls learned that Charles Rosa had been murdered—right in the Hydesville house! The ghost said that a man named John Bell, who had lived in the house before the Foxes, had slashed his throat and buried him in the cellar!

Mr. Fox believed his daughters and decided to investigate. He dug up the cellar and found human hair, teeth, and bones!

By then everyone in Hydesville—and for miles around—had heard about the ghostly rappings. One of the people who heard was John Bell himself—he was living in a nearby town when the girls made their accusation. He hitched up his wagon and rode to Hydesville right away. Bell wanted to talk to this ghost himself—but the ghost was silent whenever he tried! The Hydesville police department brought John Bell in for questioning, but he angrily denied all the charges. The police finally decided there was not enough evidence to prove he had killed anyone. They said that Margaretta and Kate Fox were just playing a prank.

By then the cottage in Hydesville was drawing huge crowds. Hundreds of people came to "hear" the talkative spirit for themselves. In 1849 the sisters went to Rochester, New York, to give a demonstration of their skills. Rappings and knockings were heard all over the meeting room. After that, the sisters were in great demand. Margaretta and Kate, along with their older sister, Leah, became the leaders of a popular new movement called spiritualism.

The Fox sisters became famous. They toured all over the country, holding séances before amazed audiences. Sometimes people would ask them questions about a friend or family member who had died. The Fox sisters always had an answer.

In 1851 a group of doctors in Buffalo, New York, attended one of the sisters' séances. The doctors said the girls were making the sounds themselves—by "popping" their knee joints! But the doctors couldn't explain why these sounds seemed to come from all over the auditorium—or how the girls knew the answers to so many difficult questions.

Margaretta got married and retired temporarily. Kate continued to work as a medium, and later Margaretta rejoined her. They remained popular for many years. But in 1888 Margaretta and Kate made a shocking confession. They admitted they had started making the strange noises to trick their mother. They had made the sounds with their toes! And what about answering those tough questions? The sisters said they looked for clues in the face of the person asking the question. Surprisingly, this hoax did not end the spiritualism movement. There were many other mediums, and people still believed in their powers.

By the 1890's, when the sisters were in their fifties, they had lost all their money. They were lonely and unhappy. There were hundreds of mediums around, and most of them were more popular than the Fox sisters. Later still, Margaretta and Kate said their confession was a lie—they had made up the "hoax" story, hoping for money and attention.

To this day, no one knows for sure whether the Fox sisters were fakes. But everyone agrees that they launched spiritualism, one of the most popular movements of the 19th century.

Eileen Garrett

Eileen Garrett was highly respected as a medium. She claimed to be able to go into a trance. Then spirits would enter her body and speak through her, almost like a ventriloquist's dummy.

Eileen Garrett was born in 1893 in a village outside of Dublin, Ireland. As a child, she felt that she was different from her friends. She had strange visions. Once she saw her aunt walking toward her with a baby. But at that very moment, her aunt was at home dying—while having a baby!

At age 17, Eileen Garrett moved to England and went to the British College of Psychic Science, a school that taught people how to be mediums. In the 1930's she traveled across the United States and England and became known as a famous ghost hunter.

One of Eileen Garrett's most famous cases was the haunting of Ash Manor. In 1936 the K. family (as they asked to be called) moved from London, England, into a beautiful old mansion called Ash Manor. Ash Manor was in a part of the English countryside called Sussex. It was a bright, cheerful home with lovely gardens. Ash Manor was not the sort of place you would expect to be haunted. But the K. family didn't know its history of bloodshed and fire, or that it was built on the site of an ancient prison.

One autumn night, terrifying groans woke up the entire family. They all lay trembling in their beds in the darkness. Suddenly, they heard heavy footsteps coming from the attic!

Every night the ghostly sounds continued. Everyone had trouble sleeping at Ash Manor. Then one evening shortly before Christmas, Mr. K. went to his bedroom to change his clothes for dinner. As he walked through the doorway, he saw a shadowy figure standing by the window. Mr. K. thought it was a burglar. He tackled the intruder, but he found himself struggling with thin air. The K.'s became convinced that Ash Manor was haunted. Mr. K. called Dr. Nandor Fodor, a well-known parapsychologist. Dr. Fodor asked Eileen Garrett if she would join his research team, and she agreed.

Within a week, Dr. Fodor, Eileen Garrett, a researcher, and a secretary traveled to Ash Manor. The group decided to hold a séance in an upstairs bedroom. When a séance is held to get rid of a ghost from a haunted house, it is called a *rescue circle.*

As they went upstairs, Eileen Garrett sensed a ghost. A chill ran through her body. The group sat around a table in the cold bedroom. Garrett closed her eyes and went into a trance—she looked as if she were sound asleep. Suddenly she opened her eyes. She said hello—but in a mysterious voice with an Indian accent!

Some mediums have spirit helpers to help them talk to other spirits. Eileen Garrett said she had more than one spirit helper, but her main one was named Uvani. Uvani was like a telephone operator. He could put Garrett in touch with a ghost. And he could disconnect the line if she was in danger! At the Ash Manor rescue circle, Eileen Garrett told Uvani about the K.'s problems. She wanted Uvani to help her talk to the ghost who haunted the mansion.

According to the séance group, Uvani told Garrett that he would connect her with the spirit. Suddenly, Garrett's body began to twist into strange, painful shapes. She tried to talk but could make only choked crying noises. The ghost of Ash Manor was trying to speak—but he had forgotten how to make words! After a few minutes, his voice became clearer and the group could understand him.

They discovered that the ghost was Lord Henley. He had lived 500 years earlier and had been imprisoned in what was to become Ash Manor. First, Lord Henley was knocked out and dragged to the dungeon by his enemies. When he woke up he began to scream, so one man cut his tongue in half! In the dungeon Lord Henley became ill, and his body grew twisted and deformed. He rotted away in the dungeon and eventually died. But now the ghost of Lord Henley was confused. He thought he was still alive!

After the ghost told his sad story to the group, he was quiet. Dr. Fodor explained to Lord Henley that he was dead. He told him his suffering was over—he could go wherever he wanted to. Suddenly, Eileen Garrett woke up from her trance. She blinked a few times, then she asked the others what had just happened. The K.'s never saw or heard their ghost again!

Eileen Garrett was always curious about her special powers. She wondered why she could talk to Uvani and others. Over the years, she let scientists study her. Some scientists tested her blood when she was in a trance to see if it was different than it normally was. They couldn't find a change. Some *psychoanalysts,* or doctors who treat disorders of the mind, thought Uvani wasn't a ghost at all. They believed Eileen Garrett had created him herself—that he existed only in her mind. But none of the scientists ever discovered whether Eileen Garrett was a true medium.

4

The Proof Is in the Picture

In 1862 a Boston photographer named Mumler took a picture of himself. But when he developed it, he saw someone else in the picture—a cousin who had been dead for 12 years! Spiritualists came from miles around to see Mumler's amazing photograph. They wanted to have pictures taken with their dead relatives, too!

Back then, photography was as new as spiritualism. Few people understood how it worked. Mumler and dozens of other *spirit photographers* took advantage of this. They used trick photography to make their eerie images. First they took an actual picture of the dead relative and pasted it onto the portrait of the living relative. Then they took a picture of their "collage" and sold it to the living relative. People were so happy to have these special pictures that they wouldn't believe they were fakes.

Raynham Hall

Almost all of the early spirit photographs have turned out to be frauds. But experts think that some modern ghost photographs are not fakes. One of these is the famous photograph of the Brown Lady of Raynham Hall.

Back in 1835 the Townsand family had invited a few guests, including their old friend Colonel Loftus, to spend Christmas week with them. They lived in Raynham Hall, a very old and elegant home in the English town of Norfolk. One evening after dinner, Colonel Loftus went to bed early. In the upstairs hallway, he saw a strange female figure gliding ahead of him. She was wearing a long dark gown. He thought she might be one of the other guests, but then he remembered that everyone else was downstairs! He took off his glasses and rubbed his eyes. When he put them on again, the woman was gone.

Colonel Loftus didn't tell anyone about the mysterious woman. But a week later, as he was leaving his room, he saw her again. Her gown was made of rich brown satin, and she walked with her head held high. As she passed Colonel Loftus, she turned to him and flashed an evil grin. Her pale face was glowing, but instead of eyes she had empty sockets!

Colonel Loftus ran downstairs to tell the others what he had seen. Some laughed, but others said they had seen the ghostly woman, too. They had kept quiet about her because they didn't want anyone to laugh at them.

Years later, the writer and Navy Captain Frederick Marryat was visiting Raynham Hall. He had heard about the Brown Lady, but he didn't believe in ghosts. Then one evening he and two other guests said they saw the Brown Lady at the end of the upstairs hallway. The ghost was holding a lamp in one hand—and coming closer and closer to the guests! The three men hid behind an open door. As the Brown Lady passed, she smiled wickedly. Captain Marryat pulled out his pistol and shot her. But the bullet went straight through her—into the wall! Then the Brown Lady vanished.

In 1936 the British magazine *Country Life* sent two photographers, Captain Provand and Indre Shira, to Raynham Hall. They were taking pictures of the beautiful old house for an article about interior decoration. The photographers set up their camera at the bottom of the main staircase. All of a sudden, Shira saw a woman in a gown walking down the stairs! He yelled to Captain Provand to snap the picture. Captain Provand didn't see anything, but he took the photo anyway. When they developed the picture later, they could clearly see a woman walking down the stairs. The Brown Lady is wearing a veil and a long dress, but you can see straight through her! To this day, no one knows whether the ghostly figure in the photograph is real. But no one can prove that it isn't.

The Tulip Staircase

Two Canadians, the Reverend Ralph Hardy and his wife, were visiting the National Maritime Museum in Greenwich, England, in 1966. (Three hundred years before, King James I had built the house for his wife, Anne of Denmark.)

When the Reverend Hardy and his wife entered the mansion, they saw the wide, curving Tulip Staircase in front of them. The Reverend took a photograph of the elegant stairway.

When the Hardys went back to Canada, they had their pictures developed. To their horror and surprise, in one photo they saw three hooded and robed figures who looked like monks climbing the Tulip Staircase! One of them was holding the railing tightly. A ring glittered on one of his fingers.

The Hardys knew they hadn't seen anyone on the staircase when they were there. What was going on? They sent the photograph to parapsychologists to try to find out if the figures were really ghostly monks. The parapsychologists sent it to photography experts who claimed the picture was authentic!

5

Poltergeist!

What is a *poltergeist?* It's a ghost that's heard or felt —but never seen. Poltergeists are noisy spirits. They thump, crash, and bang. They move furniture and throw things—they may even scream and cry. It is said that poltergeists haunt people, not places. But some scientists say that poltergeists aren't ghosts at all. They think poltergeist activity is really just a powerful energy force—like a blast of cold air, for example. This force, they say, can be created by the human mind.

The Amherst Poltergeist

One famous poltergeist case took place in Amherst, a village in Nova Scotia, Canada, in 1878. Two sisters named Esther and Jeannie Cox lived in a two-story cottage with their married sister, Olive, and Olive's husband, Daniel Tweed. Olive and Daniel's two young sons also lived in the house. Jeannie Cox was 21, and Esther Cox was 19.

Esther and Jeannie shared a bedroom. One night, as they snuggled in their beds, they began to hear strange noises. The sisters sat up in bed and listened. Knocking and thumping noises surrounded them. The sounds seemed to be coming from every corner of the room. The sisters were scared. They thought that hundreds of mice had invaded their room. But when they checked the walls and their straw mattresses, they found no signs of mice.

Two days after the noises began, Esther woke up screaming in the middle of the night. "My God, what's wrong with me?" she cried out. "I'm dying!" Jeannie and the rest of the family rushed to her bedside. Esther's face and arms were horribly swollen, and she was in terrible pain. While she screamed, a loud knocking echoed throughout the house.

After a few hours the swelling went down and Esther felt better. But the swelling returned 4 days later—and so did the noises. This time, even stranger things happened. Blankets jumped off beds. Small objects fell off tables and flew across rooms. But scariest of all was the message that was mysteriously scratched into the wall: "Esther Cox You Are Mine to Kill."

Soon everyone in the neighborhood had heard about the awful haunting. Hundreds of people flocked to the house to witness the poltergeists for themselves. The police had to come just to keep things under control.

Then Esther got so sick she couldn't even get out of bed. Daniel Tweed, Esther's brother-in-law, thought she might get better if she left the house. A man named John White had heard about Esther's problems and felt sorry for her—he said she could stay with him. Esther went to John White's house, and the strange noises stopped at the Tweed cottage. All was quiet at John White's house too—for 6 weeks. Then, suddenly, Esther's poltergeist came back. Small fires began to break out all over the house: The poltergeist was lighting matches and dropping them on the floor. It seemed to be trying to burn down the house—with Esther in it.

So Esther went home, but the fires didn't stop. There they broke out every day. To save her family and their cottage, Esther decided to leave.

She went to work as a housekeeper for a family who lived on a farm. She kept her troubles with the poltergeist a secret. But one afternoon the barn caught fire and burned to the ground. Esther told her employer about the poltergeist, but he didn't believe her—he thought she had started the fires herself. He accused Esther of arson and took her to court, where the judge didn't believe her either. He sent her to jail!

When Esther got out of prison, she met a traveling showman who had heard about her poltergeist. He asked her if she wanted to appear onstage. She had no money and no job, so she agreed. A huge audience came to her show. They wanted to see chairs flying around and fires starting. Esther walked onto the stage, sat down, and concentrated. The minutes ticked by. Nothing happened. The people in the audience became angry and wanted their money back.

Esther Cox spent the rest of her life wandering

from place to place and from job to job. She was an unlucky, unhappy woman. She believed that wherever she went, her troublemaking ghost was right by her side. But others thought Esther caused the fires and strange sounds herself. Nobody knows the truth.

Esther Cox's case is very unusual because the poltergeist activity lasted for so long. Most poltergeist hauntings last only a few months. But Esther claimed this poltergeist stayed for the rest of her life. In the end Esther's "ghost" became her only companion. She died in Massachusetts in 1912—and only then did those strange disturbances end.

6

Modern Haunted House Stories

Do you think haunted houses existed only long ago? Well, many people believe ghosts and haunted houses are still around, in cities, towns—maybe even down your street.

The Texas Terror

Not all haunted houses are old and crumbling. Sometimes they're brand-new.

In 1980 Ben and Jean Williams built their dream house in a neighborhood that was being developed outside of Houston, Texas. They'd finally saved enough money to have a home built just the way they wanted it: big, modern, tan brick.

For a short while, Ben and Jean were happy in their new home. But in 1981, strange things began to happen. Toilets flushed by themselves. The garage door opened and shut without anyone touching a button. And one night, when Ben Williams arrived home from work, he saw eerie, dark shapes in the living room. They were moving across the floor and looked almost like black clouds.

Then, one by one, relatives of the Williams family became ill. Within a very short time, four people died: Ben Williams's father-in-law, brother-in-law, grandmother, and mother. "It should have been a lovely place to live," Ben has said. "But there've been deaths, deaths, deaths ever since we moved into that house." He couldn't stop thinking that all those bad things were related to their beautiful new home—especially when Tina, the Williams's 30-year-old daughter, was diagnosed with cancer.

Meanwhile, other people were building houses in the neighborhood. And they started having odd experiences, too. One day the Williams's next-door neighbors, Sam and Judith Haney, began building a swimming pool in their backyard. But they stopped work almost at once. Why? An elderly man had knocked on their door. He told them that dead bodies were buried under their house. The Haneys wanted to know if that was true. So they rented a tractor and started to dig. Suddenly, they hit wood. The Haneys unearthed part of a coffin—with a skeleton falling out of it!

Now even stranger things began to happen. One morning Judith Haney couldn't find her shoes anywhere in the house. But she did find them outside—right in the open grave they had just dug up. Other neighbors claimed to see shadowy forms in their homes. Unplugged TV sets glowed in the dark. Some people thought ghosts were stirring up all this trouble!

The Haneys wanted to move out of the home they

had just bought. They decided to sue the company that had developed the neighborhood to try to get their money back. But they needed more information. So the Haneys talked to old people who had lived nearby their whole lives; they also did research in the library. Soon they discovered something that convinced them their house—and maybe the entire neighborhood—was haunted. The houses were built on top of an old cemetery!

The Haneys told the Williamses what they had discovered. Was their home sitting on top of graves, too? Jean Williams resolved to find out. She started to dig in her own backyard. Each day, she dug a little deeper. Then tragedy struck again in January 1987. Jean Williams had dug a hole only 3 feet deep when their daughter Tina died—not from her cancer condition, but from a massive heart attack.

Jean Williams stopped digging; she had had enough. Enough sickness, death, and tragedy. She wanted to leave that haunted house and its memories far behind.

A few days after Tina's death, the Williams family moved to Hamilton, Montana. The Haneys also abandoned their home. Bit by bit, the Williams's lives went back to normal. But they still believe there's an evil spirit in their old Texas neighborhood. And they believe they can help other people who are going through the same things they did. The Williamses have started a support group called The Other Side. They've asked people to write and share their ghostly experiences. Do you have anything to tell Ben and Jean Williams? You can write to them at P.O. Box 1386, Hamilton, Montana 59840.

Happy Hauntings

Modern haunted houses don't have to be terrifying. Some people claim they live with ghosts—and wouldn't want to change a thing!

Nancy Raiche-Osborne and her husband, Mike, moved into their house in Middletown, Ohio, in 1985. They loved the house, with its big porches, peaked roofs, and sunny rooms. But right away Nancy noticed something strange. The house had an odd musty smell. A few months later, after the birth of her son, Adam, Nancy Raiche-Osborne felt something brush against her. When she looked around, nothing was there!

As a toddler, Adam began to act as if somebody else were always in the room with him—even when he was completely alone. When he was 3, Adam told his mother he had just talked to a woman in the hallway. He said her name was Mrs. Quattlesby. Nancy Raiche-Osborne was amazed. The name of the original owner, Mrs. Oglesby, sounded much like that. Adam had no way of knowing her name. Had Adam just seen her ghost?

Nancy Raiche-Osborne felt a little strange about this. But she and her husband thought the ghost had every right to be there. They even thought the ghost might be helpful. Once, after looking for a lost ring for days and days, Nancy Raiche-Osborne asked the ghost for help. The next day she found the ring—right on top of her dresser.

Visit the U.S. Military Academy at West Point and maybe you'll catch a glimpse of Molly the phantom housekeeper or the ghostly soldier of room 4714!

For hundreds of years, England's Tower of London was the site of thousands of executions. Some believe the ghosts of prisoners still roam the hallways.

Young Edward V and his brother Richard, Duke of York, mysteriously disappeared in 1483. Many believe their uncle, Richard III, had the princes killed in the Tower of London so he could become King of England.

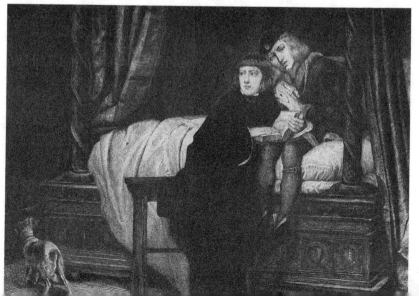

Some say that in the 13th century, a nun was buried alive on the grounds of Borley Rectory. This building burned to the ground in 1939, but the nun's ghostly presence is still said to haunt the area.

This photograph of the gateway to the grounds of Borley Rectory was taken in January 1955 by Thurston Hopkins. Another photographer took a picture at the same moment, but no ghostly figure appeared in *his* photograph!

Borley Church and cemetery.

Harry Price, who investigated the Borley Rectory hauntings, seals a bedroom window with tapes in another haunted house to find evidence of a poltergeist.

Sarah Winchester claimed she was acting under orders from her dead husband's spirit when she built this 160-room, 6-acre mansion for the ghosts that haunted her.

If you visit the Winchester Mystery House you will see this stairway that leads to the ceiling. No one knows why Sarah built such an odd house for her ghosts.

Fox sisters Margaretta (left) and Kate (middle) were the first mediums. This drawing from the late 1800's shows the Foxes with their married sister, Leah Fish.

The Fox cottage in Hydesville, New York. Some believe that the Fox sisters communicated with the ghost of Charles Rosa, a peddler thought to be murdered there.

Eileen Garrett, one of the most popular mediums in the 1930's, often spoke to ghosts with the help of Uvani, an Indian spirit.

The Lutz family house in Amityville, New York, where Ronald DeFeo killed his entire family because voices told him to do so.

In 1936 Captain Provand said he unknowingly took this picture of the Brown Lady of Raynham Hall. No one has been able to prove whether or not this spirit photograph is a fake.

7

Real-life Ghostbusters

In the movie *Ghostbusters,* wacky ghost hunters rush out to fight pesky ghosts night and day. In real life, ghosts are a little harder to track down than that. Every year, organizations like the American Society of Psychical Research get hundreds of phone calls asking about ghosts, but only a few are worth investigating. Some "hauntings" are caused by ordinary events like squirrels in the attic. Others might be made up by people who just *want* their house to be haunted. How do ghost hunters know if a claim is worth checking out?

First, the ghost hunter talks with the people who think there may be a ghost in the house. The ghost hunter wants to make sure they're telling the truth. Then, if it doesn't sound phony, an investigator will visit the house. Sometimes he or she will bring along a medium to try to communicate with the ghost. Parapsychologist-turned-ghostbuster Ian Currie of Toronto, Canada, explains, "Most ghosts don't know they're dead. They usually give me an argument." But he still tries to convince them to leave the world of the living.

Most parapsychologists use more scientific means to see if a house is haunted. Ghostbusting equipment has become very advanced. Special video cameras are able to take pictures in the dark. Sometimes the camera even has an audio recorder. The recorder can tell what direction a sound is coming from. Investigators might also use an *infrared sensor,* a beam of light that shows if something—even something invisible—passes through it. Ghostbusters also use a special device called a *thermostater* to measure and record temperature, since a ghostly appearance is supposed to bring cold air with it. Another device, called a *strain gauge,* can tell when air pressure changes. If something is slamming shut a door, for instance, the gauge will pick up the force. Even computers can be helpful.

With all this modern technology, have scientists figured out for sure if there really are haunted houses? Read on and find out.

A High-tech Experiment

In the fall and winter of 1989, a wealthy woman bought a penthouse (top-floor) apartment in a luxurious New York City building. (The exact location can't be disclosed, to protect the privacy of the people who live there.) The penthouse was on the sixth and seventh floors of the building. Mrs. P., who asked that only initials be used, was living in Europe when she bought the apartment. But when she moved to New

York, she discovered something terrifying: Many people in the building believed the penthouse was haunted.

The apartment's previous tenant had been an elderly woman named Mrs. G., who had died after a long illness. When two morgue attendants came, they accidentally dropped her body on the floor of the elevator!

After that, eerie things began happening to the workers in the building. One afternoon, maintenance men were cleaning up the penthouse apartment. The elevator opened right into the apartment, so they kept it on the sixth floor while they carried in supplies and equipment. One of the men had just finished polishing the wooden floors with a waxing machine. He started to push the heavy waxer into the open elevator, when all of a sudden the waxer hurtled down the shaft. The man lost his balance. He was starting to fall, too, when his boss rushed over and pulled him back into the apartment. The machine fell six stories and smashed to pieces at the bottom of the elevator shaft.

What had happened to the elevator? The two men looked in the shaft. They saw that the elevator had gone up to the seventh floor—all by itself—and the sixth-floor door had stayed open! An emergency repairman came and said that the elevator wasn't broken. What had happened was impossible!

Other building workers had strange experiences as well. One doorman saw a man walk through the lobby one evening. The doorman jumped up and ran to the front door to let him out. But the man suddenly vanished! A security guard in the building across the street also reported seeing strange things. Lights went on and off at strange hours in the empty penthouse—even when no one was there!

Mrs. P., the new owner of the penthouse, decided to call in a special research team. One way or another, she wanted the ghosts out of the building! This research team included four mediums, three parapsychologists, an exorcist who called herself a "white magician," a photographer, and a filmmaker.

Over the next few days, this team conducted all sorts of experiments. The research team used high-tech equipment to help them find ghosts. The photographer took pictures with an infrared camera, which, unlike regular cameras, can photograph images in the dark that people normally can't see. The parapsychologists used a special computer. The computer was hooked up to a machine with a light bulb on it. When the computer was on, the light was programmed to flash on and off a certain number of times. The parapsychologists thought that a ghost might interfere with the program and change the number of times the light flashed.

One day, the researchers set up the computer in the ballroom of the penthouse. They turned on the computer and ran their tests. Then the white magician performed magical rituals to get rid of the ghosts. She set up an altar in the ballroom and drew voodoo symbols on the floor. When she had finished, the researchers turned on the computer again. Then they compared the computer results from before and after the magical rituals.

What did the parapsychologists find out? When the photographer developed the special infrared film, he noticed strange patches of light on it! An expert from the Kodak Information Center couldn't explain it. Had the photographer taken pictures of ghosts? The researchers didn't know, but they agreed that it was possible.

And what about the computer? The light on the machine blinked slightly more often in the parts of the building that weren't supposed to be haunted. Were ghosts turning *off* the light in the haunted places? Again, the researchers didn't know. The light blinked the same number of times before and after the ritual exorcism. Did that mean that the exorcism had not worked? Or did it mean that ghosts weren't there in the first place?

This fascinating experiment didn't give Mrs. P. many answers. But it did lead the way for other studies using scientific experiments and advanced equipment. Who knows what these high-tech ghostbusters will discover next?

The Amityville Horror

Despite all the equipment available to modern ghost hunters, their most important tool is still common sense.

In March 1976 Alex Tanous and two other parapsychologists went to visit the Lutz family. The Lutzes had recently moved out of their house in Amityville, New York, claiming it was haunted. While they were living in the Amityville house, the Lutzes said, they had heard scary voices calling out to them. They told the parapsychologists that dozens of tiny "devils" had flown at them. And that a swarm of flies had got into the house and attacked them. Finally the Lutzes said they had often seen the face of Ronald DeFeo—the 24-year-old man who, just one year before, had killed his entire family in the house! At his trial, DeFeo said he had shot his family because voices in the house ordered him to do it.

Alex Tanous wanted to study DeFeo's handwriting to see if it offered any clues. The Lutzes showed Tanous the young murderer's signature—at the bottom of a contract for a book and a movie! The couple had hired a writer named Jay Anson to write *The Amityville Horror* and had also made a deal with Ronald DeFeo. They needed to use DeFeo's life story to make their book and movie complete.

DeFeo *had* really killed his family, but the ghost hunters suspected that the Lutzes had made up their haunted house stories for money. The Lutzes knew a terrible murder had taken place when they bought the house. Did they take advantage of that fact to invent those stories about the devils and the scary voices?

The ghost hunters investigated the Amityville house. They couldn't find anything unusual—except for the television crew and all the reporters snooping around! Without using any special equipment, the ghost hunters decided the Amityville Horror was a fake. Later, the Lutzes' own lawyer admitted it was all a hoax to make money. And the present-day owners agree. They say they've had no strange experiences there!

Just because the Amityville haunting was a hoax doesn't mean that all such reports should be ignored. The debate about whether ghosts exist will probably go on forever. What you *can* do is conduct your own investigation. See for yourself what's real and what's not!

8

Haunted Houses You Can Visit

Would you like to visit a haunted house? To find out if there's one near you, go to the main branch of your local library and ask the librarian if she or he knows about any in the neighborhood. The library might even have a ghost file! You could also call your local historical society or chamber of commerce about haunted house tours. If you can't find any in your neighborhood, here are some houses you can visit that have *not* been mentioned in this book. Ask your family members or teacher for help. Who knows? You might just see a ghost!

The Morris Jumel Mansion
Edgecombe Avenue and West 160th Street
New York, New York
(212) 923–8008

While visiting this 18th-century mansion, a group of schoolchildren saw the ghost of Madame Jumel, who is said to have killed her husband!

Loudoun Mansion
Germantown Avenue and Apsley Street
Germantown, Pennsylvania 19144
(215) 685–2067

Watch for the ghost of an 8-year-old boy while tour-
ing this 19th-century mansion. They say he likes to
play tricks on the tour guides!

The Whaley House
2482 San Diego Avenue
Old Town San Diego State Historic Park
San Diego, California 92110
(619) 298–2482

This is the home of four noisy ghosts. You can hear
footsteps and the rustle of clothing, and smell ghostly
cigar smoke!

The George Wythe House
Colonial Williamsburg
Williamsburg, Virginia 23187
(804) 220–7645

See the ghost of Lady Skipworth, who floats through
the house dressed in a ball gown!